CW00369656

Thoughts and Prayers
for Special Occasions

THOUGHTS AND PRAYERS FOR SPECIAL OCCASIONS

Lionel Fanthorpe

BISHOPSGATE PRESS

This book is dedicated to Dr Brian Stableford, an outstanding Science Fiction writer and one of the front rank of those whom it is a great privilege to call my friends, to all of whom pages 67 and 68 are especially addressed.

© 1992 Lionel Fanthorpe

British Library Cataloguing in Publication Data
Fanthorpe, Lionel
Thoughts and prayers for special occasions.
1. Christian life. Prayers — Devotional works

All rights reserved. No part of this publication may be reproduced, stored in a retrieval system or transmitted, in any form or by any means, electronic, mechanical, photocopying, recording or otherwise, without prior permission of the copyright owner.

All enquires and requests relevent to this title should be sent to the publisher, Bishopsgate Press Ltd, Bartholomew House, 15 Tonbridge Road, Hildenborough, Kent TN11 9BH

Printed by Whitstable Litho Printers Ltd., Millstrood Road, Whitstable, Kent

Contents

Foreword

What persuades people to write books? The work involved is considerable and critics abound. Dr. Johnson was in no doubt of the answer:-

"No man, except a blockhead, ever wrote except for money." Some, no doubt, write in that hope, but few make their fortune. Only the very gifted, or the very lucky, ever attain to the best seller.

Others write as scholars. They have reached a level of knowledge in some particular field of research or learning and long to share their researches with others. These are the authors of the standard text book, the definitive work in their subject, and no student worthy of the name would dare to sit an examination without first having read their books.

More often than not, writers exist simply to entertain. The book, in a sense, is their stage. They know what they write is no great work of literature and will be as ephemeral as most, but they will rest content if they can find a public to amuse, to mystify, or even to frighten.

For the few the call to write is more of a vocation, and is part of a wider ministry. It is just one of the ways in which they can serve others. The good nurse in a hospital will be similarly driven, but her compassion will be expressed through her hands, her spoken words, her calming presence. She will be doing all she knows to allay the fears of her patients, of pain or loneliness, or of the unknown, and replace them with courage and hope for the future. The good public servant, similarly, will show his compassion by seeking to remove obstacles that oppress the lives of defenceless people and free them from irritating injustices, generally easing their passage through life as best he can.

Clearly there are many ways of helping others and writing is just one of them. Such a writer the Reverend

Lionel Fanthorpe has now surely become. In one of his earlier books in this same series, "Thoughts and Prayers for Troubled Times", he sought to share the lives of the anxious and the depressed, not merely highlighting the causes of their sadness, or the pain of it — they could have done that for themselves — but leading them gently towards the things that heal, indicating some of the secrets by which their inner hurt could be redeemed. There was, and no doubt there always will be, compassion behind his pen. In this book, however, very differently, he is trying to examine with his fellows some of the happy, enriching experiences that over the years have come their way, hoping as he does that no one will see them, so to speak, as theirs by divine right, as if they were the lot of all people all the time, but always to see them as special, as something to marvel at, and in the process leading at least to the beginnings of gratitude.

The birth of a baby, to use one of his themes, is in one sense not all that remarkable. It happens all the time, all over the world. Babies are born to rich and poor alike. But it is special; it is a miracle every time it happens. Ask any childless couple what the birth of a child would mean to them. There are, in fact, books in plenty that help us to deal with our many sadnesses. This book seeks to persuade us not to disregard our joys. It is a book of love written by one who has an overwhemling gratitude for the many good things that have come his way in life. He is for ever conscious of the love and kindness and friendship by which his life has been enriched. He writes in the hope that others may realise equally how fortunate they are, how strangely blessed they have been, and, like him, go on to thank God for it.

Canon Stanley Mogford, M.A.

Introduction

Every day is a special occasion. I was attending a short course at Leeds University when I met a marvellous old Economics Lecturer who greeted us all with a cheerful smile and said: "I'm going to enjoy talking to you today. Over twenty years ago my Doctor told me I had only a few days to live. So I wake up grateful every morning; I look in the mirror and say, 'Well, I'm still here!' " For him every day was a special occasion, an unexpected pleasure. Life was a daily renewable joy, a series of bonuses which he hadn't really thought he would receive. His whole attitude to daily living was influenced by his awareness that it was up to him to make the most of life . . . day by day.

Even when we cultivate the very healthy philosophical attitude of my old friend in Leeds and try to make every day a special occasion, there are still some days that must by their very nature be *extra special*. A child is born; someone gets married; we change jobs; we retire; we move house; we win an election; there is a birthday or an anniversary; we go to a party; we enjoy a Beethoven Symphony; we buy a new bike; we win a race; we make a wonderful new friend; we fall in love.

In my other volumes, I have set out to suggest ways in which God — and very often God alone — can help us through troubled and lonely times, so it is a great joy to lay before the reader a few ideas about sharing our happiness with the God of Happiness.

One of the kindest and most active Parish Priests I ever knew was Canon Noel Boston of Dereham in Norfolk. He was above all things a particularly *happy* Christian with a magnificent sense of humour. His

God, like C.S. Lewis's God, was a God of Great Joy. Being with Noel for a few minutes was enough to help his parishioners to experience that joy too. His happiness and his goodness were infectious.

The father of the Prodigal Son rejoiced. The woman who found her precious dowry coin rejoiced. The shepherd who found his lost lamb rejoiced. Christ tells us to rejoice. Christianity is the happiest of all faiths. In Jesus our Saviour, God gives us eternal and abundant Life. The heart of the Gospel is that God loves and cares for each one of us so much that He would have gone to the Cross for you and you alone. The heart of the Gospel is that God cares, that His love is Infinite. The heart of the Gospel is that God wants us to be unimaginably happy with Him and with all those whom we love for the whole of eternity. It is amazing. It is breathtakingly wonderful — and it is *true*! Surely then, this Father of Love and Happiness wants to share with us the Joy He gives us. He is not only there to pick up the pieces and comfort us when life goes wrong, or when we have done something particularly stupid and sinful, He is there to share our joy and to celebrate with us, when we use His gifts aright and experience some of the gladness that he wants us to have.

Lionel Fanthorpe
Cardiff, 1990

A New Baby

When it happens, the clichés are no longer clichés —just some well-worn and inadequate attempts to express the miracle. We say that he or she — the new arrival — is exciting, wonderful, beautiful, cute, sweet, adorable . . . and so on, and so on. And, of course, every poor, overworked word is true. We mean them all. We are like the poor man invited to the feast at the Manor House with nothing to wear except one shiny, threadbare, old suit. It's not good enough for the occasion, any more than our poor old baby-praising cliché is good enough for the occasion — but it's all we've got, so it'll have to do. Poets can rise to the occasion with phrases like 'trailing clouds of glory' but the finest poetic phrases are so far from our true feelings that they're very little better than the deeply expressive cooing noises that loving grandmothers and wise old aunts make on these occasions.

The more deeply we think about the event, the more wonderful it is: not only has a new human being come to join us here on earth — this tiny, helpless, miniature person is a prospective son or daughter of God. This is one of those precious souls which Christ came to save for an eternity of joy. We are not rejoicing for a new mortal with some seventy or eighty earthly years to look forward to: we are rejoicing for a new prospective Citizen of the Kingdom of Heaven with unlimited potential in an unlimited Future with Christ. This is cause for celebration indeed!

Poem

There are no words which can express
The wonder and the loveliness
Of this small person smiling here:
So sweet, so new, so very dear.

"Hello, young miracle," we say,
And for your future we will pray
That long and happy years you'll live
And that to Christ your heart you'll give.

You were not born for earth alone.
You'll stand with us before Christ's Throne.
Tiny immortal, yours shall be
A joyful, endless destiny.

Prayer

Almighty God, Creator and Sustainer of the Universe,
You were born as a Baby at Bethlehem when You came
to earth to save us. Father of All, You once came among
us as a Child — help us to see You in every babe. Grant
us the wisdom and love to raise this child as You want
us to do. Help us to show this baby the love of God in
the lives of family and friends. May this child grow up
to know You, to love You and to serve You faithfully
on earth and in heaven. May all this baby's potential
be realised in the life of a good, happy and fulfilled
adult. We ask it for the sake of Jesus Christ our Lord.
Amen.

Baptism

One of the best definitions of a sacrament is that it is the outward and visible sign of an inward and spiritual truth. A great tragedy of Christendom, and apparently one of Satan's more successful ventures, is the way that the followers of Jesus argue and quarrel over what they mean by a sacrament. It is only the inward and spiritual truth which matters. If a grimy and travel-stained Christian in a waterless desert was asked to baptize an equally ragged convert by trickling a handful of warm sand across his brow, I have no doubt at all that provided baptizer and candidate sincerely *meant* what they said and did, their version of the Sacrament of Baptism would be just as acceptable in the eyes of God as a ceremony conducted in the noblest cathedral in the world by immaculately robed, fully ordained and universally recognized Bishops and Priests with the candidates in their crispest white starched gowns, and Holy Water drawn from the Jordan itself! It is good, right and proper to use every appurtenance we have available — but the trimmings without the true repentance and the faith in Christ's forgiveness are worse than useless. They are what a luxuriously laid table in a foodless restaurant is to a starving man.

When the inward and spiritual part is right, how we can rejoice at the Sacrament of Baptism for infant, child or adult. Here is a baby, a boy or girl, a man or woman, coming to God to say: "Lord, I am sorry for my sins. I believe in You and in what Your Son, Jesus Christ, has done for me at Calvary."

Here is a person who has come to Christ to say: "I truly repent, and, with Your help, I intend to do my best to be a Christian from now on." The Holy Angels themselves rejoice in Heaven when those thoughts spring truly from a human heart, or, in the case of infant baptism, from the hearts of those who have brought the baby to join Christ's Church.

Poem

The sacred promises are made
From the repentant heart,
And then with Christ, the King of Kings,
Abundant Life can start.

Godparents all, and loving friends,
Parents and sponsors true,
Rejoice in what Baptism means
To the baptized and you.

Let all who seek to serve the Lord,
Small child or adult strong,
Enter by Water and the Word
To join the heavenly throng.

Prayer

Loving Heavenly Father, we know because Jesus taught us, that children are especially welcome in Your Heavenly Kingdom. Bless all sincere and penitent candidates for Holy Baptism, their Godparents, sponsors, parents, families and all who help to prepare and welcome them, for the sake of Him who was Himself baptized by John in the Jordan, Jesus Christ our Lord. Amen.

Confirmation

In those churches which practise infant baptism, confirmation provides an opportunity for the young adult, or the child who is old enough to make real decisions, to do what sponsors and Godparents did during the candidate's early infancy.

An important decision is always a special occasion. Our wills, our knowledge of our own self-hood and our intentions about what to do with it, are the quint-essence of our very being. Life is a complicated entanglement of choices and forks in the road. We choose a marriage partner; we select a career; we opt for one sport or recreation rather than another; we decide whether to save or spend; to invest in one company rather than another; to take a holiday here rather than there ... Each in its own way is an important decision, but the importance is relative. A good holiday is not as vital to us as a good career or a good business; a good marriage with a loving partner is infinitely more precious than being at the top of a lucrative profession. Being right with God is the most important choice of all: there is no neutral position. There is no fence to sit on. It is God or Satan; Christ's way or the world's way; Heaven or hell. Confirmation is making the right choice. Confirmation is the act of an independent mind saying "Yes" to God our Father, and having that positive response publicly recognized by the Church. Making such an important right decision is a very special occasion, and a great cause for celebration. Confirmation is a prominent landmark on the road to Heaven: it is indeed a joy to reach it.

Poem

They did it for me, long ago,
When I was small and new.
I couldn't make decisions then,
Or ponder what to do.

But now my will and mind are clear;
I'm able to decide,
So I confirm the choice they made:
I'll serve the Crucified.

On this my Confirmation Day,
I make my stand for God.
Let Saints and Martyrs guard the way —
I'll seek the path they trod.

With God to guide my wayward feet,
And hold my erring hand,
For Him Who bore the Cross for me
Today I make my stand.

Prayer

Lord Jesus, You were always a Man of Decision during Your time on earth with us. Bless my decision to be confirmed; help me to be faithful all the days of my life. Guide me on the Christian path I have chosen. Help me to be of use to others. Help me to lead others to You, so that they, too, can make the right decision for themselves. I ask it for Your Name's sake. Amen.

Engagement

Big decisions have to be made carefully. We buy a house, often the biggest purchase of a lifetime, in thoughtful and deliberate stages. A deposit is paid. Contracts are exchanged. Completion comes later. So it is with marriage. After our commitment to Christ, a loving and lifelong commitment to another human being is the biggest and most important decision we are ever called upon to make. We usually do that in stages too, although 'whirlwind' romances are not unknown, and often turn out just as well as the long and carefully planned ones.

Engagement is an important milestone on the road to marriage, but it is a milestone that is set at a crossroads. It is not a final and irrevocable commitment. It is an opportunity to say: "At this stage of our relationship, and as far as I know my own feelings now, I think that you and I would be happy together in marriage." It is an honest statement of intent — nothing more. Circumstances change. People change; intentions change; feelings change. It is infinitely better to have second thoughts during your engagement than a few days after the wedding! Despite that word of caution, an engagement is a very real cause for celebration. We are declaring in front of all our friends and relations that we regard each other highly enough to want to get married. We are making a statement about sharing and planning together. Opening our lives to others is always a good thing. Just as Divine Love is freely open to us, through Christ, so God delights in our human life-sharing. All true fellowship, companionship and sincere love for others is in harmony with the Divine Will.

Prayer

Dear Lord, our Heavenly Father, the only Source of true and perfect Wisdom, our only worthwhile and reliable Guide, help us to understand the seriousness and importance of getting engaged as well as the joy and wonder of it.

Help us to be absolutely certain that this life-long Christian marriage which we are planning together is what we really want.

Let us please You first and then ourselves.

Do not let us be persuaded or influenced by the ideas and expectations of others — however well-intentioned they may be.

Make us true to You first and then true to ourselves.

We ask it for the sake of Jesus Christ, our Lord of Love, Truth and Honesty.

Amen.

Marriage

Male and female created He them. That which God hath joined let no man put asunder. It is called marriage: it is wonderful, mysterious, among the most ancient of God's Holy Ordinances and yet as fresh and new as the happy young couple whom their Priest married this morning. Undertaken seriously and reverently and with a full awareness of its awe-inspiring seriousness, it is as important a life-event as birth or death. None of us chooses to be born, and very few of us deliberately choose to die, but marriage is up to us. The third of the three mighty life-events is ours to choose, and what a momentous choice it is.

I have already made many wrong decisions in the course of a long and eventful life, and unless the Lord's Second Coming or my own death intervenes, I shall undoubtedly make many more. I have made only three decisions in the last half-century of whose absolute rightness I am unshakeably certain: to accept the Christian faith unreservedly; to seek and be accepted for Ordination as a Priest; and to marry Patricia in 1957.

Marriage is a very special occasion indeed: sharing the rest of your life — and every part of your life — lovingly and sensitively with the right partner is the nearest thing to Heaven which this earth affords. Realising too late that you've both made a terrible mistake and that you're fundamentally incompatible could mean living in one of hell's most sinister anterooms for a very long time, enduring the refined misery of being chained to someone who has become an implacable enemy.

Poem

Three landmarks dominate the map of life,
Three lofty peaks that dwarf the market place:
The first is birth — in which we have no choice.
The next is death — in which our choice is small.
The third is marriage — where our choice is all.

Two questions make or mar our fleeting days,
Two mountain crests that challenge our ascent,
The first is God or Satan — faith or doubt?
The second is the partner we invite
To share life's journey — we *must* choose aright.

One answer only: one throw of the dice —
Indelible the ink within life's pen —
One arrow may we aim at each great mark:
Christ or the world? Whom shall I wed, and when?
Once burnt, this bridge cannot be built again.

Prayer

Loving Heavenly Father, You instituted marriage and
the sacred mystery of love between men and women.
It is by Your will that we seek one another, marry and
love one another. Bless all our decisions. Guide us
aright. Fill us with Divine Love so that our earthly love
may also be richly blessed. Be at our wedding and
bless us as You blessed the wedding at Cana. Stay with
us throughout our lives together; keep us true to You
and true to each other, for the sake of Christ our Lord.
Amen.

A New Home

That wonderful old song "Bless This House" is not heard today as often as it ought to be. The once widely prevalent custom of blessing houses is not practised as often as it used to be, and we are poorer both for the loss of the song and for the loss of the blessing.

Moving into a new home is a very exciting thing, as well as an exhausting experience. We don't realise at the outset just how much there is to pack: unless we've had the experience several times! I've lost count of the number of times we've moved since 1957, but Patricia hasn't! From Dereham, to Wymondham, to Gamlingay, to Romford, to Boxford, to Lyng, to Hellesdon, to Cardiff . . . Where next? we wonder. Curtains, carpets, bookshelves (always the dreaded bookshelves!) everything has to be sorted, adjusted, modified and rearranged. But the exhaustion doesn't quite overtake the excitement — at least it hasn't yet.

A new home brings many other new things with it: a new Church, a new Parish Priest, a new neighbourhood to explore, a new paper-shop, a new butcher, a new baker, a new grocer . . . new friends to make, new jobs to do, new things to learn. I can well remember my first few weeks in Cardiff when I dared not leave home without my A-Z street map in the car in case I couldn't find my way back!

And yet in all that bewildering newness, God's love is constant, steadfast and dependable. Every new home we have is a good home, as long as we recognize Christ as its real Head.

Poem

We've finished wrapping china,
And it's all inside the crate.
They promised to be here at nine —
They're certain to be late.

The cats are at the cattery,
And the dog is in the car —
I hope he won't be sick *again*:
It really isn't far.

The 'phone is disconnected
So we cannot make a call:
The public one's been vandalised —
It's hanging off the wall!

The Gas Board said they'd call today —
I don't know if they will.
There's so much stuff inside the car
It won't go up this hill!

Once everything's been sorted
We'll be happier than before —
But how I dread these next few days
Of boxes on the floor!

Prayer

Creator Lord of all new things, help us to settle in our new home and to be happy here. Help us to make new friends and to find worthwhile new things to do in Your service in this new place, for the sake of Christ our Lord. Amen.

Retirement

The ageing process is particularly susceptible to the constitution, personality and will-power of the individual. There are nonagenarians with the twinkling eyes, mischievous humour and effervescent energy of perpetual schoolboys. Any sensible employer would benefit greatly from having them on his payroll. There are teenagers and young people in their twenties whose lassitude and torpor are so massive that only an abnormally early pension could save them from destitution. Admittedly, these are extreme cases, but they do exist, and as long as they exist, retirement ought to be very flexible.

Scripture abounds with episode after episode in which great leaders defied the years and carried out God's work superbly well at a very advanced age. There can be no better precedent than Holy Scripture.

Many people long to retire, and look forward to it: calendar and wishes coincide — that's fine! A glorious sunset and a long, long golden evening lie ahead. This is something to celebrate, a special occasion to mark and enjoy, a case of "Now, Lord, let Thy servant depart in Peace, according to Thy word . . ." (to paraphrase the *Nunc Dimittis* from the Book of Common Prayer).

The most important thing of all is to remember that we never retire from the service of God. Working for Christ is not merely a life-long commitment in earthly terms, it is an *eternal* contract: it is a life-long covenant in *everlasting* terms. We are His *forever*. All that we have ever done during our so-called 'working' lives prior to our 'retirement' has been of secondary importance compared to our service for Christ. It is only our

secular work which ends at retirement: our *real* job —
our true reason for living —our service to Christ —
never ends.

Poem

Another milestone reached;
A day's march nearer home:
"Retired?" Perhaps, yet full of life:
A long way yet to roam!

Another milestone passed:
Yet many lie ahead.
I'll show them that the word "retired"
Does *not* mean "nearly dead"!

God's Patriarchs of yore
Were twice as old as I —
Yet they achieved amazing things:
And I shall ere I die!

God, keep my mind awake;
And this old body strong —
Give me another task for You,
And that shall tune my song.

Prayer

Loving Heavenly Father, Timeless and Ageless God of
past, Present and Future, help me safely to pass this
milestone called 'retirement'. Show me that I am
always of worth in my Father's eyes, even if there are
some people here on earth who no longer seem to
want me. Point me to new horizons of worship and
service, and let me still serve You by serving others, for
the sake of Christ my Lord. Amen.

A Holiday

The longer we've waited for a holiday, the more enjoyable it seems to be. If financial or domestic circumstances have made it impossible to get away for a year or two, how much more we enjoy our holidays when they do eventually arrive.

Holiday, of course, originally meant 'holy day' and our medieval ancestors — like some of our brothers and sisters in lands where the Church is still influential in secular society — kept more holy days than we do.

What is the best way to keep a holy day? What would God our Father have us do with the day he has given us, the holiday he has given us? The first characteristic of love is that it seeks the joy and welfare of the beloved. There is no greater love than God's love for us, no greater expression of that Divine Love than Christ's sacrifice on Calvary, His ultimate enactment of the distance that Love is prepared to go on behalf of the beloved. In small things and great, God our Father, Christ His Son, and the Holy Spirit want us to be joyful.

Christianity should be the happiest and most radiant of all religions: God, the all-powerful and all-loving Father wants us — you and me — to be happy with Him forever. It is so magnificently simple that it is almost impossible to grasp: yet it is the true heart of the Gospel. Having a happy, refreshing holiday is part of God's loving will for us.

The Ten Commandments are not gloomy and threatening prohibitions: they are a guidebook showing the way to true happiness — if we put God first, and care lovingly for one another, earth verges on Heaven. If we follow Christ's Two Commandments (which brilliantly summarise the Ten) we find again the perfect formula for happiness — loving God and one another not only ensures a happy holiday, it ensures a fulfilled and happy life.

Poem

I live in the mountains: I long for the valleys.
I live in the desert: I long for the sea.
I live on the plains: and I long for the hill-side.
I live in the fens: how the forests call me!

I live in the city: I long for the country.
I live in the country: I want city fun.
I live in the tropics: I long for cool breezes.
I live with cold winds: how I long for hot sun!

It isn't the place: it's the feeling and longing,
The seeking and questing, for somewhere that's *new*,
For something exciting, for something that's *different* —
Remind us, dear Lord, that we're searching for *You*.

Then anywhere, everywhere, *allwhere* is perfect:
The Kingdom of God is around and within —
With You, blessed Lord, as our God and Our Father,
The best of all holidays has to begin.

Prayer

Most loving Heavenly Father, we thank You for the many joys which our holidays bring. As we travel to see other parts of this wonderful world You have made for us, help us to see more of You in Your creation. As we meet new friends in faraway places, help us to show them Your love, and help us to find You in them as we enjoy fellowship together. We ask it for the sake of Christ our Lord. Amen.

Starting a New Job

Although I've been a professional writer for nearly forty years (I marketed my first story in 1952, and I've sold about 200 titles since then) and, therefore, like to regard authorship as my main profession, I think I may also claim with all due modesty to be something of an expert in starting new jobs! Mark Twain is alleged to have said, "It's easy to give up smoking: I've done it hundreds of times." I think as far as jobs are concerned I know how he must have felt!

I started my working life as a dental technician immediately after leaving school in 1950, and *so far* I've been: a machine hand in a clock factory, a farm labourer, a barber, a journalist, a grocer's van-driver and warehouseman, a traffic clerk, an electricity board storekeeper, a Corona driver-salesman, a secondary school teacher, an examiner, an industrial training officer, a Cambridge University Extra-Mural Board Tutor, a Company Director, a Comprehensive High School Headmaster and a Priest! I'm confident that the next fifty years will be equally full, interesting and varied! When I wish the reader every blessing, happiness, and success in his or her new job, I can honestly claim to know a little of what it feels like to be starting something new!

A new job is a new opportunity, and, naturally enough, we want to do well at it. Rest assured that God our Father knows exactly how we feel. Trust Him. He will help us through all this newness and strangeness, and make all things turn out well for us. He loves us more than we can ever understand. He wants us to be happy. He wants things to go well for us, and He has the power to make them go well. What more could we ask?

Poem

I began in a lab with false teeth on a slab;
I've stacked barley and hay on a farm;
I've trimmed whiskers and hair, driven vans here and
  there,
And I don't think I've taken much harm!

I've examined and taught; stocks and shares I have
  bought;
I have lectured, and tutored and trained;
Been in charge of a school; had a Company to rule;
As an Anglican Priest been Ordained.

When you start a new task, there is so much to ask:
What goes where? Who does that? Is this right?
So uncertain you feel that you need nerves of steel
To subdue your inaugural fright!

Be assured God is there, both to love and to care.
There is nothing which He doesn't know.
Put your trust in the Lord: He's as good as His Word;
Have no fear: God is running the show.

Prayer

Almighty and most loving, caring Father, I have just
started this new job: I don't know what to do; I don't
know where to go; and I'm not entirely sure what they
expect of me. Please help me, most loving and caring
Lord. I want to do well here. I want to be an asset to my
employer. I want to feel that I'm genuinely pulling my
weight and earning my wages. Help me to understand
things quickly. Calm my anxious nerves and racing
heart, for the sake of Jesus Christ, my Lord. Amen.

Promotion

Promotion is a great compliment, a great boost for the ego, a great tonic for the self-confidence: being passed over when we thought we should have had the promotion is more painful than a kick in the stomach. Yet we should not feel like that because promotion is a strangely arbitrary thing. It is more often the result of being in the right place at the right time, than of any great merit, skill, wisdom or virtue on the part of the promotee. History has produced its share of Cabinet Ministers, Generals, Bishops and Captains of Industry who did not deserve to be left in charge of a whelk-stall — and there are whelk-stall proprietors who could undoubtedly run a country, an army, a Diocese or a factory, with confidence, skill and success. It is often whom you know, rather than what you know that results in promotion. It is an image (true or false) which gets promoted more often than the man or woman who wears it. Therefore, let us temper our delight in promotion with a little realism. Many a cunning and ostentatious villain has been promoted above the head of an effective but unassuming hero; many a ruthless and machiavellian confidence trickster has overtaken an honest and worthy rival. Selectors are often blind. God is not.

There is only one promotion which really matters; there is only one promotion which has any validity at all: promotion in the Kingdom of Heaven.

Am I honestly doing what I sincerely believe to be God's will? Am I seeking to love and serve Him first, my brothers and sisters second, and myself last? Have I accepted Christ as my personal Saviour? Have I brought my many sins to him, truly repented, and unreservedly sought his forgiveness? If I can truthfully answer those questions in the affirmative, then I have all I shall ever need on earth or in Heaven.

Poem

I filled in application forms, and told my referees;
I made a careful note of my diplomas and degrees;
I went up for the interview — that was a ghastly
    strain —
Now, after all that effort — I'm promoted once again!

I'm going to a bigger job, in charge of greater things,
My salary is higher — my career has sprouted wings.
But I must take a firmer grip upon my soaring mind —
And think about the colleagues whom I have to leave
    behind.

Promotion isn't cleverness, experience nor skill.
A lot of it is only chance — now there's a bitter pill!
The people I've just beaten were at least as good as I:
We often lose to lesser men, no matter how we try!

Lord, save me from my boasting; help me curb my
    stupid pride.
My ego's a pathetic thing, Your dying love beside.
Lord, I'm glad I've been promoted. Help me do my
    new job well:
But Lucifer was filled with pride the moment that he
    fell!

Prayer

Most merciful Father, forgive me if I am unduly proud
of this promotion. Help me to understand the deep
truth of C.S. Lewis's teaching that we must learn to
love our neighbours as ourselves before we are
allowed to love ourselves as much as we love our
neighbours. Help me always to remember that promotion doesn't often have much to do with merit in
this world. Teach me to value Your approval only, not
the empty and ephemeral approval of earth, for Jesus'
sake. Amen.

Starting a New Business

What does it take to start a business? What do you have to be to become what the economists love to call an entrepreneur? You need a streak of stubborn independence; a lot of courage; a fair helping of imagination; plenty of stamina and endurance; reasonable flexibility; a rational mixture of optimism and realism . . . and that mysterious quality called 'flair' or 'business acumen'. Unfortunately, I can't tell you specifically what that is: I can recognize it when I encounter it, but I can't define it accurately enough to advise you how to acquire it, or to improve what you've already got. It's a certain kind of personality style, a particular type of rare talent: I suspect that the best entrepreneurs are born rather than made.

To be a Christian entrepreneur requires something in addition: an absolute determination never to let 'business ethics' replace Christian ethics. There are special temptations which lie in wait for Christian businessmen and women which their non-entrepreneurial brothers and sisters are not exposed to. If your tax is deducted from your wages via PAYE, you don't have the temptation to make questionable expense claims. If you're simply taking cash at a till where all the prices are decided and marked up by other staff, you aren't subject to the temptation to mark up an unreasonably high profit because the customer is ignorant of the item's real worth. In the same way, if you're a knowledgeable antique dealer in business on your own, you may be tempted to offer an ignorant seller a small fraction of what you know a valuable piece is worth.

Poem

You need an independent streak, a lot of courage too.
A good imagination is invaluable for you.
A boiler full of stamina will stand you in a good
    stead —
And the vital flexibility to go where you feel led.
You need to be an optimist with a pragmatic line —
You also need another thing, which I cannot define.
Some call it 'business acumen' and others call it 'flair':
Unless you've got that vital spark, you won't get
    anywhere!
Above all, as a Christian, never let your morals slip —
Temptations are more trying when you're captain of
    the ship.
You've got decision-making power: it's yours and
    yours alone —
But one day all must answer when we stand before
    God's throne.
So let each Christian business head be moral, kind and
    fair:
God is the Final Auditor Who bids us all take care.
Entrepreneurs, remember, for it is our Lord's decree:
"What you have done to others, you are doing unto
    Me!"

Prayer

God of all Justice, Lord of all Fairness, bless our
business dealings and always keep us honest. Make us
Christians first, and entrepreneurs second, no matter
how much we enjoy business life and competition.
Remind us to give good measure, and to charge only
what is fair. Teach us to care for the poor and the
underprivileged, the widows and orphans, the
deprived and the handicapped. Make us magnanimous
in all our dealings, ready to offer more and to settle for
less, for the sake of Christ our Lord. Amen.

Celebrating Birthdays, Anniversaries and New Year

We often speak and think about the wheel of life, economic cycles, the rotation of the seasons and so on. Things come round again and again: each one renewed and slightly different from its predecessor. We celebrate birthdays: our own, our families', our friends'. It is a very worthwhile cause for celebration. We can thank God for another year together, another year of fellowship and love shared, another year of progress and development.

It is the same with anniversaries: the founding of a Club or Society to which we enjoy belonging; the anniversary of our Wedding; the anniversary of a Priest's Ordination, or his First Celebration of the Mass. These are important dates to remember, and it is good that we should be reminded of them. Memory is the carriage that conveys us back to the event itself: the anniversaries are the milestones along life's way; Fellowship and Love are the horses which draw the carriage for us.

Birthdays and anniversaries are both public and private events: family birthdays belong in a special way to that one loving family; wedding anniversaries belong to that special bride and groom, their family and friends. But New Year Celebrations are different: they belong to everyone who shares that culture and who marks that particular New Year on the same day. New Year is something for us all to join in: it is a community event. We can look forward and we can look back together. We can learn from past mistakes. We can make new resolutions. We can go forward confidently as a united people with God as our Guide.

Poem

It turns and turns again, life's silent wheel,
And we, the riders, mark its every turn
With birthdays and with anniversaries.
New Year strolls past and pushes us along.
It is not so for God; He's Lord of Time,
Ancient of Days, Great Wheelwright of the Wheel.
He views it from His own eternity,
Where endless aeons are an evening gone.
All time's the same to Him: nothing is lost.
Past, present, future — all obey His Will.
His Will is love and goodness, joy and peace
For us forever. One day time shall cease
Yet we shall live with Him — eternally.
Then we shall know as we are known; and learn
The mysteries of time which He conceals:
We'll see our anniversaries as steps
Upon the road to Heaven's endless bliss.

Prayer

Lord of all time and of eternity, Father of every
universe that was, and is, and is yet to come, help us to
understand the real significance of birthdays, anniversaries and New Years. Master of time, teach us to
understand what it really is, and help us to use that
share of it which You have given us in the best possible
way. Teach us to spend it wisely: in worship and in
loving service to our brothers and sisters; in prayer
and meditation and the planning of good works; in
giving happiness to others and in enjoying our own
lives, for Jesus' sake. Amen.

Welcoming a Grandchild

What a beautiful little milestone you are! How you've changed your parents' lives, and mine! I can still remember quite clearly a few vivid episodes in my own infancy, long before I went to school, things that happened when I was only a couple of years older than you are today — and now, with bits of my own childhood still very much alive in my memory, I'm a grandparent! It takes a lot of getting used to: I'm not sure that I shall ever fully understand it. Like many of life's mysteries and wonders, being a grandparent is something we can enjoy without fully comprehending. It is part of the infinite mercy and love of God to place delights and wonders before us — and you, young stranger, are a *great* delight and wonder — which we can ponder for a lifetime, enjoy hugely, but never fully fathom.

My new grandchild is a wonderful little telescope through which the eye of my imagination can catch glimpses of the future. What will the world be like when you're as old as I am today, eh? Will you fly to Mars for a holiday with as much nonchalance as I fly to London? Will you have a computer built into your wristwatch that will communicate by satellite with anywhere in the world? Will the politicians have got rid of poverty, homelessness and disease for us?

I know one vital fact about the future: God will still be here. He will faithfully love and guide you and your generation as He has always loved and guided me and mine. Whatever the future has in store, He will be there. I have nothing of value to leave you except my faith. Take it now. Make it your own as soon as you're old enough. It will serve you well.

Prayer

Father and Maker of all life, bless and protect our new grandchild. Make us worthy of this great responsibility. Help us to reveal Christ to this new person whom you have entrusted to our family in all we say and in all we do.

Make us into signposts which point unerringly towards You.

Grant us the joy of watching our grandchild grow up, and the privilege of giving any help we are invited to give.

Grant us the gladness of loving fellowship across the generations, so that we may be real brothers and sisters in Christ — regardless of the differences in our ages — as well as being grandparents and grandchildren.

We ask it for the sake of Jesus Christ our Lord, Who existed before Abraham was born, yet lay as a Babe in Mary's loving arms, and Who understands and blesses all children, and the family life of their parents and grandparents. Amen.

Winning an Election

It's over. The last vital vote has been counted. We've won. I've been elected. I'm the new Secretary, the new Chairman, the new Councillor — perhaps even the new MP. It's over at last, and we've *won*! I'm so happy, so thankful and so relieved. It was a tense and trying time. I can't pretend I enjoyed it. Things were getting a bit vicious, and there were some unpleasant personal attacks flying around in certain quarters. I tried not to get down to that level. I tried to win the argument, not the exchange of abuse. I don't think a Christian candidate ought to go in for personal abuse tactics, but it's very hard not to retaliate once the other side has started it. Oh, well! It's all over — at least until the next election.

The thing to do now is to concentrate on keeping the promises we made. I only hope we can. That's even worse than descending to mud-slinging — failing to keep the promises. That's what gives politicians at every level a bad name. The voter gives a cynical grin on the doorstep when you're canvassing and says: "You're all the same! You'll promise me anything today, and forget me as soon as you're safely elected!"

It's up to politicians of all parties and at all levels of government to keep faith with the electorate: if we don't we're letting down the principle of democracy itself — and that's courting national disaster.

The important thing isn't so much winning the election as keeping faith with your voters and maintaining your integrity afterwards.

Prayer

Lord of all justice, fairness and mercy, supreme ruler and organiser of this limitless universe, I thank You for my victory in this election. My new powers and responsibilities are infinitesimally small beside Yours, but they are far greater than those I have had before. Help me to use them, aright. Save me from the stupidity of pride and pomposity. Remind me always that I am the privileged servant of those who trusted me enough to elect me — not their master. As Solomon, Your servant, once prayed for Wisdom, so, in my much smaller sphere, I also ask for the precious gift of Your Wisdom now: not for myself, Lord, but so that I can be of more use to Your people.

I ask it for the sake of the best and wisest Leader of all, Jesus Christ, my Lord.

Amen.

Writing, Painting, Composing Music

Creativity is the word. Our Father is the ultimate Creator, the sublime Author, the perfect Maker and Sustainer of all that is. Holy Scripture itself tells us that we are made in His image. In our own smaller way, we are creators too. He lets us share with Him in this breathtakingly exciting work of creation.

When a teacher helps a student to understand some new fact, or to acquire a new skill, part of creation's work is taking place. When a poet brings images, rhyme and metre together to convey a new idea, or to shed new light on a familiar theme, that, too, is part of creation. A skilled painter with brushes, pigment and canvas is emulating his Heavenly Father's example. When an author welds plot, characters and setting into a novel, God's work of creation is being furthered. A musician composing symphonies and sonatas is also doing God's work.

When we lift a brush, guide a pen, or strike a note we are involving ourselves in God's work of creation.

Creative talent can be used in various ways: sadly, not all of them are good. Literacy can compile prayers or pornography. The same painter's brush can depict beauty or brutality. A musician can compose a concerto or an advertising jingle persuading the gullible to waste scarce resources on useless, tawdry trivia.

If human creativity is to follow the example of Divine Creativity, it must be indissolubly linked to morality and integrity. Let us write; let us paint; let us make melody: but let us always do it responsibly and to the glory of God.

Poem

The poem and the play; the mighty speech
That forged and built a nation's destiny;
The novel that ten million of us read;
The symphony that every ear has heard;
The colours hanging in the Louvre for this
Dark world to view with rapturous gaze;
Composers, artists, authors, poets all,
Extol and worship God in what you do.
Only your best, your *very best*, will serve;
The Master Hand you copy is Divine.
And seek no rest, for there is work to do.
Stoke up imagination till the sparks
From your small fires to Heaven's gate ascend.
Lay words and music, colour, shape and form
Upon the Altar of that generous God
Who gave you every talent you possess.

Prayer

Lord of all creation, Father of beauty, harmony and
meaning, inspire and direct all artists and writers, all
poets and playwrights, all composers, choreographers
and musicians. Let every form of art be filled with
goodness and beauty for Your glory, O great Creator,
and for the good of all mankind. Help us to resist every
temptation to misuse our talents — for You have most
generously given different creative gifts to each and
every one of us. Help us to discover and to use rightly
what You have bestowed upon us. Help us always to
enjoy and admire the works of others, and thank You
for their talents more than for our own. We ask it for
the sake of Christ Jesus, our Lord. Amen.

Going to a Party

Getting invited to my friends' birthday parties was one of the most exciting things that happened to me during my infant school days, that and inviting them to mine. We played the usual infants' games; we ate jellies and sausage rolls, trifle and ice cream; in our own simple way we enjoyed ourselves immensely.

As we grew older, we still enjoyed parties to some extent, but they were different affairs somehow: the magic of infancy was fading. Many cynical and sophisticated adults give the impression that they would rather avoid parties if they possibly could without giving offence. 'There'll be the usual ghastly get-together at Quentin's again this year: I suppose we really have to go?' The voice is languid, the expression bored and supercilious. It is ironic to think how offended the speaker would be if ' ghastly Quentin' (who probably has the misfortune to be related to her) didn't invite her!

Jesus said that unless we become like little children, we cannot enter the Kingdom of Heaven. As always, He was absolutely right. Unless we can recover the simplicity, the honesty and the directness of children, we shall shut ourselves out from the only party that's really worth attending — the Divine Feast in the Kingdom of God. We need to make deliberate effort to re-kindle our youthful enthusiasm. Quentin's parties would not be ghastly if people went there with the intention of being nice to poor old Quentin and to all their fellow guests. If we set off with every intention of being bored, we shall be. If we are determined to be happy, we shall be. The heavy burden of choice is entirely ours.

Prayer

Restore to us, most loving Father, the simple joys and enthusiasms of our childhood. Teach us to relish parties and every other opportunity to be in fellowship with others, to serve them for Your sake.

Help us to see that in the Mystery of the Holy Trinity, the Fellowship of the Transcendent Godhead is Perfect Love and Perfect Unity. Teach us that the closer we come to one another in loving fellowship and sympathetic understanding here on earth, the closer we come to You, our God of Perfect Fellowship.

As we go to this party, Lord of all true Joy and Pleasure, fill us with the determination to be loving, kind, helpful, thoughtful and unselfish to everyone we meet there, so that they will enjoy themselves because of us.

May they see in us something of Christ, the Perfect Host and the Most Welcome Guest.

We ask it for His sake.

Amen.

Going to the Theatre or Cinema

We live in many worlds: our work, our church, our family circle, our dreams ... and the worlds of art, drama, theatre and cinema. God has given us such lively, exploring, inquisitive minds that we — like the Athenians whom St Paul encountered in the Book of Acts — are always anxious to see and hear 'some new thing'. We cannot change as often as we might want to the real world routines with which we so quickly and easily become bored: but we can find some of the newness we crave in the theatre or cinema. The play may be an old favourite, a Shakespeare or a Sheridan that we have already seen a dozen times, but each interpretation is different and surprisingly fresh. The film may be enjoying its premiere tonight. It may be the work of the most imaginative, *avant garde* producer this century has yet seen: still it will not completely satisfy our deep hunger for something genuinely *new*. It is only in God Himself that that yearning is fully satisfied. He Who is older than time is newer than tomorrow. Only in the Infinity of Love and Wonder that is God our Father can we find enough real freshness to keep us happy forever. Everything else becomes stale and boring eventually.

As we go out with family or friends, with just one loving companion, or by ourselves, to enjoy the experience of theatre or cinema — or even as we settle to see a new video at home — we should remember that the God-given longing for new and exciting things is one more signpost which He has put here on earth to indicate our way to Heaven. All newness, except the amazing newness of God, will grow stale sooner or later.

Prayer

God of the Morning, Lord of Creation, Planner, Instigator, Initiator and Maker of all things new, help me to understand this hunger within my soul for something different, for something fresh, for something novel, for something I've not seen nor heard before.

Help me to understand that this burning desire for newness comes from You, and that I can never fully satisfy it until I turn to You, its Source: the ever-flowing Fountain of all that is truly new.

We thank and praise You, Lord of Creation and Creativity, for every good film and every good play that is there for us to enjoy in the theatre and the cinema, and especially for the one we are just going to see. We praise and thank You for the writers, directors, producers, actors, artists and musicians who give us wholesome and refreshing entertainment on stage and screen. Thank You for the pleasure that comes from the entertainment they provide, and for the happiness that comes from visiting places of entertainment with our families, friends and loved ones. We offer our thanks and praise in the name of Jesus our Lord. Amen.

Staying with Friends/Entertaining Friends

Jesus Himself often stayed with friends. He was a frequent and welcome guest in the home of Lazarus, Mary and Martha at Bethany. He went to the home of Zacchaeus, the unpopular tax collector. When a prospective disciple asked where Jesus lived, the Lord said, "Come and see." He fed the 5,000 who had followed Him to hear His message of salvation. He was Host at the Last Supper, and washed the disciples' feet (the work of the lowliest slave) in that sacred upper room. After His resurrection He broke bread in the house of Cleopas and his unnamed friend at Emmaus. Jesus sets us a great example of hospitality and visiting. He puts the divine seal of approval on our human social life. He made us social beings. We need one another. We need fellowship, friendship and love.

When our Lord sent His disciples on their preaching tour He gave them rules to ensure that they would not inadvertently take advantage of anyone's hospitality. When others came to Him for hospitality, He invariably gave magnanimously: He changed water into wine; He turned a handful of loaves and fishes into a feast for thousands; He gave His life itself for the salvation of us all. By everything He said and did, Christ taught us that in all our entertaining and visiting a host should be generous, a guest should be grateful and appreciative.

Let us go with joy to the homes of our friends and family; let us welcome them with gladness to ours. Let us open our doors and spread our tables for the lonely and the needy, that in so doing we may emulate the example of Christ our Lord.

Poem

Friendship, Love's more cautious, gentle cousin,
Smiles and beckons to us warmly.
"You are welcome in my home, old friend."
"And you, my known and trusted companion,
You are welcome in mine."
We were at school together.
We toiled at a grimy bench together.
We have driven together through ice and fog.
We have shared traffic jams and crowded commuter
    trains.
Your classroom was next to mine,
And we kept an eye on each other's pupils
With the door ajar, while one of us made coffee.
Your house was next to mine, and each of us kept
    guard
While the other was away on holiday.
Now I am coming to stay in your home;
And you are coming to stay in mine.
It will be good fellowship again.
We shall talk of old times and old places;
We shall reminisce incessantly,
Borrowing unashamedly from each other's fading
    memories;
And thus, carefully, we shall pile more good clean coal
On Friendship's heart-warming fire.

Prayer

Loving and merciful Saviour, Friend of sinners and
constant Companion of the friendless, bless all these
warm human friendships You have given us. Make us
good and loyal friends, true to You and to one another,
for Your Name's sake. Amen.

Spring Cleaning/Re-decorating

The wonderful riverside adventures of the Toad, the Water Rat, the Mole and the Badger in the children's classic *"Toad of Toad Hall"* could be said to have begun with the Mole's spring cleaning of Mole End, and his unwillingness to get on with the tedious task of white-washing the place. Whether in fact or in fiction, spring cleaning and re-decorating truly deserve to be called Special Occasions.

In our vigorous application of clean, fresh paint and wallpaper to surroundings which have slowly grown dingier and drabber than we can tolerate any longer, we have a parable of our lives themselves — not just our homes.

We all need a moral and spiritual spring clean from time to time. The heart, the mind and the soul need to be purified, brightened and freshened up periodically: and that task is of far higher priority than the simple cleansing of our homes.

We are all familiar enough with the household equipment available at the local DIY shop: but how familiar are we with its spiritual equivalent? We need God's help to peel away our old veneers of selfishness, and the dirt of many sins. Household dirt can be very stubborn — I've used steel wool on old saucepans for what seemed like hours without having much visible effect on whatever it was I'd managed to burn on! Sin is even harder to remove from the ruined fabric of a burnt out life. There is one infallible tincture, and one alone: the cleansing Blood of Christ; the Divine For-giveness from the Cross; and the Reconciliation which Jesus offers freely to all. The spiritually cleansed and renewed person is infinitely lovelier than the most beautifully cleansed and re-decorated home.

Poem

We've measured up and bought the paint,
The paper and the paste,
The calculations must be close —
We don't want too much waste.

We've taken all the curtains down,
And dusted everywhere;
We've laundered all the covers
On the sofa and the chair.

It all looks so much brighter,
And more pleasant than before —
You somehow feel more welcome
When you step inside the door.

But what about the occupants?
We need spring cleaning too!
The dust and dirt of selfishness
Leave marks on me and you.

We need the cleansing power of Christ
To make us fresh and new —
There's nothing that He can't repair:
There's nothing He can't do.

Prayer

Lord of all that is fresh, pure and good, please cleanse
and renew us again by the power of Christ our Lord.
Amen.

A New Bicycle/Car/Boat

Forty years and more after the event, I still recall the joy and excitement I felt as a boy when Mother bought me a new bike. With similar joy and excitement a few years later, I can remember riding my first motorbike, a very old BSA 500 for which I paid £15. It seemed like a lot of money in those days! Some time later I acquired my first car: a tank-like Austin 14 saloon, made in 1932. I was a journalist in those days, in charge of the Cromer Office of *The Norfolk Chronicle* and I still recall with great nostalgia and pleasure the sheer *fun* of driving that massive old machine over the North Norfolk roads in search of stories for my paper.

There is an undeniable thrill in acquiring a new bike, a new car or a new boat. I believe that thrill is God given and part of the pleasure which our loving Father longs for us all to enjoy all the time. The trouble with human beings is that they so often stain that good, simple, innocent and healthy pleasure — which our Father means us to enjoy — with the taint of pride, the rust of greed and the corrosion of envy. To enjoy the new possession for its own sake is absolutely fine: to enjoy it because it seems to put us alongside Mr Jones, or even to transform us into the enviable Mr Jones, is not quite so innocent. The pure and simple desire to relish and enjoy something for its own sake is from God. The desire to flaunt it originates elsewhere! To want to show some lovely new thing to our friends, to share our rejoicing with them like the shepherd who found the lost sheep, or the woman who found her lost dowry coin, is perfectly acceptable: we should always rejoice in one another's happiness and success. *Showing* and sharing is fine: showing *off* is the temptation we must learn to resist!

Poem

Something more than chrome and leather:
You and I belong together.
Every inch of your design
Makes me glad that you are mine.

Polished with such loving care
Till you're shining everywhere:
And each time I take a trip
Sweet the joy of ownership!

Is it pagan, thus to feel
Fondness for a piece of steel?
Letting my emotions dwell
On a gleaming plastic shell?

We must always have a care:
Of idolatry beware.
Never give a piston rod
Glory that belongs to God!

All things in proportion are:
God comes first, then man, then car.
From His Truth we cannot drift
Counting all things as His gift.

Prayer

Loving and most generous Heavenly Father, Giver of
every good and perfect gift, Fountain of all true
pleasure and of all real happiness, grant us the grace to
enjoy what Your love has provided, to share it with
our brothers and sisters, always to use it aright and to
give You the glory, for the sake of Him Who is Your
Greatest Gift to us, Jesus Christ our Lord. Amen.

Overcoming a Problem or Difficulty

Since the days of Job, philosophers and theologians have attempted to find answers to the problem of why our loving and all-powerful God allows us to struggle and suffer. From time to time, the most perceptive minds have seen a few gleamings which they have passed on to help the rest of us. One such shaft of light has been the idea that it is struggle which strengthens and develops us. If there were no weights to lift, we should never develop muscles. If there were no mathematical problems involving tensors, or numerical integration, our intellectual capacity might well remain at the nursery level. If we never had to wrestle with our consciences when we knew perfectly well that what we wanted so badly was wrong, our moral and spiritual development would be stunted. Without struggle, we would be physically, mentally and spiritually weak. Our Father most certainly loves us: because He loves us, He wants us to grow up to become His adult sons and daughters, not to spend eternity playing with rattles and soft toys in our prams. Struggle has its rewards, too.

Suddenly you find, after the twentieth fall, that you can ride a bike. After the hundredth attempt you do learn how to reverse a large car into a tight parking space. After three or four goes at a difficult examination, you get your diploma. After the accident that left you unable to walk, you finally take a few painful but triumphant steps. After many careful years of doing without, you manage to pay off some crippling debt and start to live again. The joy of eventual success is the reward that follows the struggle. We should thank God not only for His help in enabling us to scale the mountain, but for giving us the mountain to make us strong in the first place.

Poem

The sea is vast, Lord, and my boat is small;
The road is long, Lord, and the mountains tall.
The caves are dark, Lord, and their stone is cold;
Oh, grant me courage, Lord, and make me bold.

The water's deep, Lord, and the waves are high;
I fear to live, yet fear much more to die.
Give me Your Strength, Lord, help me overcome:
Secure my hand, Lord. Lead me safely home.

The debt is great, Lord, my resources small;
Help me keep working till I've paid it all.
The sun is hot, Lord, and the labour grim.
Show me my Saviour; help me be like Him.

Teach me, great Lord, that as I struggle on
I build a strength that lasts when tasks are done.
When I have conquered this, Lord, by Your Grace,
Help me to see it as my training place.

Prayer

Thank You, Lord, for every problem and difficulty which I have overcome with Your help. Help me to understand the struggles of this earthly life as things which strengthen me. Sustain and reinforce me, gracious Lord, so that I never give in, never give up, never run away. Bring me back to the battle, replace my weakness with the strength of the Holy Spirit, and bring me to new victories, for the sake of Christ my Lord, Who overcame all things for my sake. Amen.

Finding Something Important

Jesus told us how the shepherd rejoiced when he found the sheep, how the woman celebrated the recovery of her lost dowry coin, and how the loving father made merry when the prodigal son came home.

It is so frustrating when we cannot find something we need urgently. We ransack the house. We try to remember where we last saw it. We retrace our steps. Sometimes that kind of reconstructional technique works and sometimes it doesn't.

It may not be anything tangible that we have lost: it might be the technique for doing a particular job. Which keys do I have to press, and in what sequence, to make my word-processor give me more lines on a page? How do I put more paper in the magazine of my photo-copier? If I am taking a service at a neighbouring church because their Priest is ill, whereabouts do they have the collection and the notices? Do they have their hymns in the same places that we do? It's a great relief when the church-warden or choirmaster arrives and you can find the answers.

Wise old librarians often display a notice saying "A book misplaced is a book lost!" It is particularly irritating to want to show a chosen passage from a familiar work to a student during a tutorial and then to find that the book is not where you thought you always kept it! The converse is equally valid. It is a great joy, a great cause for celebration, to find something which was misplaced, or to retrieve something which was lost. Finding something important is a very special occasion indeed, and we should invariably thank God for it.

Prayer

Lord Jesus Christ, You came to seek and to save that which was lost: help us to find the things that really matter. We rejoice because something that is very important to us has been recovered. We give all thanks and praise to You that it has been found.

Help us to find the Most Important Things of All: help us to find You, Your peace and Your everlasting love.

Help us to find one another, to find our brothers and sisters, Your sons and daughters, and to bring them with us when we come to You.

Help us to find our true selves, the selves You made for us, and gave to us, so that we could enjoy abundant and eternal life with You and those we love. We ask it for the sake of Your precious Name. Amen.

Planting and Cultivating a Garden

It may be only a bowl of hyacinth bulbs on the shelf in my study; a little window-box; a moss-lined basket hanging over the door. It may be so long and wide that I need a garden tractor and a motor-mower to cope with it and hold back the encroaching jungle-wilderness. It may be a 'normal' family garden in front of and behind a modern 'semi' in suburbia.

The shape and the size are unimportant: it is my garden. It is the wonderfully exciting laboratory which God has given me to work in and make my experiments as one of His enormous team of human gardeners.

Whatever the sophisticated modern cynics may consider to be the oldest profession, I still think it's gardening: Adam was a gardener. If we think deeply about the implications of man's first relationships with God in Eden, we learn a great deal about freedom and responsibility. A garden — as big as Eden or as tiny as a window-box — is full of choice. What shall I plant here? How shall I tend it? How can I cultivate it to best advantage? What can I do with soil and seeds to serve God's plan of adding beauty and delight to His world?

Planting a garden is a very special occasion. Watching buds open and blossom spread is a very special occasion. Gathering apples and pears, strawberries and plums, is a very special occasion. Bringing the first fruits of our labours to God in thankfulness and praise in the good, old-fashioned Harvest Festival tradition is another very special occasion.

Our gardens teach us three lessons: all good things come from God; man's purpose is to work with God; and man's duty and privilege is to praise, thank and worship God.

Poem

Thank You, my God and Father, for messengers in
    green,
For leaves and stems that proclaim Your presence,
Your design, Your sustaining power and Your eternal
    love.

Thank You, my God and Father, for messengers in
    gold,
In crimson, white and blue, and every rainbow shade,
To tell me of Your beauty and Your glory unsurpassed.

Thank You, my God and Father, for the excitement of
    my garden,
For the privilege of working in it as Your gardener,
Teach me to love as well as tend our plants.

Thank You, my God and Father, for the opportunities
My garden gives me to return some tiny fraction
Of all You've given me, as simple tokens of my
    gratitude.

Thank You, my God and Father, for the chance to share
The fragrance of the flowers, the taste of fruit,
With birds, and bees, and human friends I love.

Prayer

Thank You, most generous Creator and Sustainer, for
all that You give me here in this garden. I praise You for
the good earth that nurtures the plants, as You nurture
me. I praise You for the roots that quench their thirst
here, as I quench my soul's thirst in You. I thank You
for the beauty that I see here, because it speaks to me of
Your Infinite Beauty. Amen.

Buying and Caring for Pets

Acquiring a pet is a very special occasion. To take on the responsibility of caring for one of God's creatures is a serious matter. When God made us the leaders and masters of creation, it was to care for and protect, not to exploit, the animal kingdom. What we have so lamentably failed to do so far for the earth as a whole, we can do in our own small sphere of activity as pet owners.

Our first responsibility is to love them; if our affection is deep and genuine, there will not be much wrong with the way we care for them.

Our second responsibility is to be consistent and faithful to them. You can read a book and put it down. You can watch a programme and turn off the television set afterwards. You can drive a car until you're tired of it, and then part-exchange it for a different model. Pets are not like that. They have their own personalities, their own feelings. They cannot be casually discarded or neglected like inanimate objects. We have an inescapable moral obligation to them for life.

Our third responsibility before acquiring a pet is to ask ourselves whether we can face up to the inevitability of losing it. *It hurts.* The death of a dearly loved pet is a very real category of bereavement.

A Priest is often asked by sad animal lovers what he thinks about the possibility of meeting our pets again in heaven. *I am quite certain that we do.* I believe that God loves us so much, and wants our happiness so much, that His infinite Power and Wisdom will provide for us to have all that we love with us in His Everlasting Kingdom.

Just as magnetism runs through a chain of suspended pins, so love runs from God through humanity, and from human beings to the animals they love. As Christ's Perfect Love conveys endless and abundant life upon us, so even our weak and imperfect love draws our pets into His Kingdom with us.

Poem

Oh, purring shape of sleepy, friendly fur
Contented on my knee, or by my side,
Lapper of milk, and connoisseur of meat,
Mysterious the dimensions where you hide!

Lolloping, eager, shaggy, clumsy dog!
You've knocked the coffee table down once more!
What future now, passed pawn on bishop six?
Kings, knights and rooks are rolling round the floor!

I might have won this game without your help.
Things looked quite good before your intervention.
Is this another of your crafty schemes
To bring your food and walk to my attention?

I stroke a silver nose, and stir bran mash,
Polish a saddle and adjust a girth.
I really don't know why I love you so —
The stoutest, slowest pony on God's earth!

Prayer

Thank You God my Father for all the animals in Your Creation, and especially for our pets. These lovely creatures are Your gift. All Love is Your gift; help us to love them even more; grant us the skill and patience to bring happiness into their lives. Help us to be their friends as well as their owners. From the simplicity and faithfulness of animals, help us to learn more about the nature of love, for the sake of Jesus Christ our Lord. Amen.

Academic Achievements

All academic achievement is relative. The boy or girl with serious learning difficulties who eventually struggles through to achieve the lowest available grade in some simple, local school-leaving certificate has done more than the gifted man or woman who romps away effortlessly with scholarships, top honours, distinctions and post-graduate qualifications.

The parable of the talents is quite specific on this point: the man who has most gifts is required to do most with them. God's standard of achievement for us is that we shall all do our very best: nothing else is acceptable at all. The standard is absolute. If you have the kind of mind that will win you a Ph.D., go out and get one. If you have the kind of mind that will win you just one solitary GCSE subject at the lowest possible pass grade, go out and get one. If you can pass an IQ test at the Mensa level — do it. If you find if difficult to spell two-syllable words, or multiply three by five and get the right answer — learn to spell *'effort'* and *'success'* and memorize the whole of the five times table. In God's eyes that makes you a Nobel Prize winner.

Whatever our level of academic achievement, let us praise and thank God for it. He gave us the intellect to accomplish it. He gave us the courage, stamina and determination to see it through. He gave us the loving family and friends who always helped and encouraged us. He gave us the concerned, skilful and friendly teachers, tutors and lecturers who helped us through the course. Let us rejoice and give thanks for our success, and give the fullest credit where it is due.

Poem

Those anxious, weary days and months and years,
Preparing for exam after exam.
It seemed that there was nothing else in life:
All I had time for was to cram and cram.

Revising, memorizing, working late,
And rising early, while the skies were grey.
Now it's all over, and the prize secured:
I've passed! I've got it! I have won the day!

"I've got it!" did I say? Was that my boast?
God gave the mind and stamina that won.
Was I alone in all those battling years?
God gave the loving friends who helped me on.

God sent the teachers and the tutors all,
To help me analyse and understand.
God gave the parents, husband, daughters, sons,
And loving wife to hold a tiring hand.

It's God's success, and theirs, not mine alone.
So praise and thanks once more with all my heart.
We have achieved *together* this great thing,
And mine has really been the smallest part.

Prayer

Thank You, most generous Father, for this success in
my examination. Thank You for giving me the ability
to understand it, and the stamina to keep going while I
was learning. Thank You for the loving family and
friends who supported me, and for the teachers, tutors
and lecturers who explained things to me. Help me to
share my joy with them, to acknowledge what they
did for me and to thank them properly. Amen.

Recovering from Illness or Accident

God is Life. God is Love. God is Health. God is Perfection. God is the Source of all healing, all recovery and all regeneration. When we have recovered from illness or accident, it is God whom we must thank. God wants us to be whole and well. We are His beloved sons and daughters, His children, His creation. His will for us is entirely good.

The research scientist who invents the medicine, the physician who prescribes it, the pharmacist who mixes it and the nurse who administers it are all doing God's will. Each is an important link in His chain of healing.

Sometimes the healing is instantaneous and miraculous, as it was when our Lord Himself healed the sick during His earthly ministry. The blindness, the deafness, the paralysis, the fever, the leprosy . . . are driven away as though they had never been. Whether God works through the sudden and mysterious power of spiritual healing, or through the slow, careful skill of scientists, doctors, pharmacists and nurses, our recovery is equally in harmony with His will. God loves us and wants us to be well, whole and happy.

When we co-operate with God's healing will by using our own determination to get well, and our faith in His healing power, we are like a sensible oarsman rowing with the tide, or a glider pilot following the best winds and rising on the strongest thermals. And when, as now, we have recovered, let us be thankful. Only one of the ten cleansed lepers came back to thank Jesus. Let's emulate his example. We never really appreciate how good life is until illness or accident robs us of our powers for a time. Let us thank God not only for our recovery, but for the quality of life which it has re-opened to us.

Poem

Sing praise to God on high,
For making all things new.
My health and strength are now restored:
All thanks, dear Lord, to You.

Through danger and through pain,
Your hand has led me on,
Yours was the strength that held me up
When all of mine had gone.

The night of sickness fell,
I could not see my way.
Your lamp of Grace drove darkness back,
My path was clear as day.

The weakness now has passed;
For joy I shout and leap,
As though I newly had awaked
From deep, refreshing sleep.

You gave me back my life;
I offer it to You —
Lord, show me my allotted task,
And teach me what to do.

Prayer

Thank You, great Lord, for healing and restoring me. Teach me to appreciate this great gift of life, and to use it in Your service and the service of my brothers and sisters, for Christ's sake. Amen.

Paying off a Debt

They are fortunate indeed who have never been in debt: they are also extremely rare. Most of us have at one time or another struggled to escape from a mountain of debt that seemed to overwhelm us and discolour everything else in life. It requires tremendous effort, stamina, resolution and strength of character to dig your way out of a debt-mountain. But when the effort has been put in, the sacrifices made and the very last penny paid off — then the sense of relief, of achievement, of freedom, of the opening up of new vistas of possibility is wonderful.

Life seems to start again. It is like a new birth. Jesus used the very meaningful analogy of debt in several of His teachings: He helped His listeners to understand the problems and dangers of sin by comparing it to the problem of monetary debt with which so many of them were familiar.

If it feels so much better just to get rid of ordinary earthly debt, how infinitely more wonderful must it feel to get rid of moral and spiritual debt?

The normal bankruptcy procedures of contemporary society — even the most sympathetic and humane of societies — still leave some sort of real, or imagined stigma on the unhappy person who has gone bankrupt. Legally and administratively the debt problem has been dealt with, but the wailing ghost remains: the clanking of its chains can echo persistently down the years.

It is not so with Christ's *total obliteration* of our debt of sin: the cleansing, the expiation, the perfection of the New Start with Him is absolute. We really are born again.

Paying off our earthly debts is a great cause for celebration — a very special occasion. Having Christ clear our debt of sin and accepting His forgiveness is the most special occasion of all: that's the one that makes the angels rejoice with us.

Poem

At last! It's paid! It's finished! It has gone!
I can't believe it after all these years
Of hardship and of scraping to get by —
I'm free again. No more frustrated tears!

My debts are paid; no more red envelopes;
No letters that begin, "Dear Sir, Unless . . ."
Final demands, nor cold, curt legal threats:
No seizures, no distraints and no distress.

It's really, truly paid: the ghost is laid.
The weight has lifted: shattered is my chain.
No more this dragging, trailing handicap —
The bills are paid, and I can live again.

Thank God a thousand times for such relief:
Our Liberator and our Saviour came.
But infinitely deeper praise we give
Because He paid our debt of sin and shame.

Prayer

Blessed Saviour Christ, we praise and thank You for clearing our earthly debts, and for the joy of being able to make a fresh start. We praise and thank You at an infinitely deeper level for coming to earth to die for us and so to pay those debts of sin which we could never have paid for ourselves. Help us to accept Your forgiveness, rejoice in Your love, and make the most of this everlasting freedom You have won for us. Amen.

Athletic and Sporting Achievements

I was just one year old when the magnificent Jesse Owens won his four gold medals in the Eleventh Olympiad in Berlin in 1936, where he ran the 100 metres in 10.3 seconds and the 200 metres in 20.7 seconds. It was well over half a century ago, but his achievement lives forever in sporting history. Jesse is almost as famous for his humorous but exquisite sprinter's prayer as for his brilliant athletic ability. Referring to those flying feet of his, he said: *"Lord, You pick 'em up – I'll put 'em down!"*

There's a lot more than humour in that gem of a prayer which Jesse gave us. It's vibrant with eternal truth and deep theological insight. It says so much about the real relationship between God and man. It acknowledges God's existence as a matter of course, as a basic fact of the universe. It recognizes difficulty. It asks for God's help in overcoming it. It recognizes that although we must put all we can into an enterprise, the greater share of all our success is God's doing.

All athletic and sporting achievement is a great source of joy and a real cause for celebration. It is a wonderful thing to compete and win. There is nothing wrong with competition as long as it's fair, clean and honest. There is certainly nothing wrong with achievement. Victory is a very special occasion. We have every right to be euphoric about it, but we need to keep close to the Owens mentality. Jesse had exactly the right approach, and his prayer expressed it. Athletic achievement is magnificent, but always remember to thank God for your success, and to give Him due credit for making your muscles so powerful, your co-ordination so good, and your reactions so fast.

Poem

This is the moment I was training for;
The striving and the struggling were worthwhile.
I've won! The battle's over! This is it!
Now comes the cheering and the victor's smile.

Euphoria: I bask in sunlit joy!
Relish the moment; make each second dear;
Stretch every minute to a golden hour,
And make the day seem longer than a year.

Keep Truth as pleasure's noblest, honoured guest.
Never forget the Source of triumph's flood.
Remember that when we have done our best
The Maker of all victories is God.

Here in our hardest sports on field or track,
In wrestler's fiercest strife or boxer's blow,
We do but model that Eternal War
Where Christ, our Champion, laid the Dark One low.

That was a Warrior's victory indeed —
Your soul and mine, and all the world's for prize.
Thank God our Champion won His Great Event:
And leads his ransomed team-mates to the skies.

Prayer

Lord of all Victories, Champion of Champions,
Supreme Commander of the Warrior Hosts of Light
before Whom all evil must fall, thank You for my
athletic and sporting successes. I acknowledge the
gifts You gave me that made my victory possible, and I
lay my success at Your feet as a thank offering. Most of
all I thank You for the Great Victory at Calvary, which
brings life to us all. I offer this, my prayer, in the Name
of Him Who won that Victory, Jesus Christ my Lord.
Amen.

Making New Friends

During the last half century I have come across only four things which we can discover, or create, in this world which continue with us, or which we find again, in the Eternal World: the first is worship, the second is character, the third is a loving relationship, and the fourth is true friendship. All four rank among God's greatest gifts to humanity. He teaches us to worship Him. He helps us to form the right sort of character. He brings loved ones together. He unites friends.

Making a new friend, or being re-united with an old one after a long period of separation, is a special occasion.

Friendship is a matter of joyful giving and glad receiving. We give each other our time. We share our thoughts, our hopes, our fears, our dreams, our everyday trivia, sandwiches and cups of tea. We explore the mental, physical and spiritual universes together. We talk and speculate about unsolved mysteries and the meaning of life. We worship together, pray together, and read God's Word together. We help each other. We encourage each other. We sympathise with each other. We console each other and bear each other's burdens. Above all, we just like being together. A friend is a truly wonderful person. We must thank God for him or her, cherish and protect him or her, stay faithfully close and loyal to him or her.

God loves our friendships. Satan detests them. If he can do anything to cause a rift or a coolness between two old friends, he will. We must guard our friendships like treasure. Protect them with warm, helpful, encouraging words. Reinforce them with little acts of thoughtful kindness. Strengthen them with unselfishness and revitalise them with courtesy.

Poem

You call me friend, and so you honour me.
There is no better title to bestow.
Christ called us friends: His Saints are Friends of God.
I call you friend in turn, and so I pledge
To do my best, despite my human faults,
To be a worthy, true and loyal friend.
No mere acquaintanceship, no morning nod,
No formal smile when I come to your shop,
Or hail your taxi in the market-place.
Such things are good, but small. Like glowing sparks
They may at length enkindle friendship's fire,
But of themselves can only hint at warmth,
Not furnish it. I must have more than that.
A universe of smiles and nods and waves
Is but a churchyard filled with well-kept graves!
It hints at buried souls that sleep and wait
For friendship's resurrection trumpet call.
Thank God for friendship: seize His precious gift
And make it ours in this world and the Next.

Prayer

Friend of sinners, Companion of the lonely and the
lost, we thank You for the glorious gift of friendship,
for the capacity to know one another as friends here on
earth, and for the divine assurance that all sincere
friendships grow and continue in Heaven. Teach us
the true meaning of friendship. Help us to be good and
loyal friends, and to find and keep good and loyal
friends, for the sake of Him Who is the truest Friend of
all, Jesus Christ, our Lord. Amen.

Falling in Love

Friendship is comfortable and warm; it glows like a coal fire on a stormy winter's night. It is a good and welcome thing, but it is controllable, and there is an air of reassuring tameness and domesticity about it.

Love is incandescent. It is brighter and wilder than lightning. It is an acetylene torch that cuts our old discrete personalities apart and welds them together into a new, united, breathtaking form. Love is ecstasy. Love is unimaginably powerful. Love conquers all things — even death. None but God Himself can control and wield it. It is His very Essence: its freedom is infinite; its dynamism has no end. Love makes universes; spin the galaxies across the heavens; sets the stars in their places and drives their planets around them.

Love leaps over erupting volcanoes, climbs icy crags, dives to the deepest ocean bed, challenges and slays the fiercest dragons . . . or quietly lays down its own life without a second thought to save the life of the beloved.

Falling in love is falling into God, experiencing as much as a human being can of the Divine Nature. Pure love is the highest rung on that mystical ladder of spiritual experience which gives us as clear a view as human eyes can stand of what heaven is like.

Of all our Father's gifts — like His gift of free-will, from which all true love is inseparable — love is the most precious and the most dangerous. That which grants us a glimpse of Heaven, can plunge us into the darkest abyss if we misuse it. The human love of lovers who put God first is like Elijah's chariot of fire — something sent by God to bring us to Heaven. Human love which attempts to deny that God is its One True

69

Source, eventually poisons and corrupts itself and dies in bitterness and destruction.

Poem

And what is love?
And where is love?
And Who is Love?
The Voice of Voices answers:
"I am Love. Find Me and you have All."
"Where are You, Lord?"
The trembling human voice,
Part hope, part fear, part wonder,
Dares to ask.
"I fear Your answer,
Yet I fear the silence more."
"I am the Living Power
Who fills all Ages and Dimensions,
And overflows the whole of Space and Time.
Fear Me — a loving fear —
And fear nought else.
Love never hides from those who truly seek."
The love we know on earth,
That lifts the heart and soul to Heaven's Gate,
Is sent from Him.
Rejoice in Love, in endless, boundless Love.
Wade in its crystal sea.
Swim through its towering waves:
For Love is Life.

Prayer

Lord of all love, all goodness, and all joy, grant us the courage to open our hearts to the delights You long to give us. Help us to overcome all fear and hesitation so that we can commit ourselves unreservedly to You, and to one another, for the sake of Christ, the Lord of Love. Amen.

Christmas

Christmas, the Birthday of the Son of God, must rank alongside Easter Day, when He conquered death, as the special occasion of all special occasions. If ever a race of created beings had a cause for celebration this must surely be it. When something of massive importance happens in our lives — we pass a final examination and qualify for a profession; the person we love agrees to marry us; a son or daughter is born — we have difficulty at first in taking it in. The greater the good news, the harder it is to realize it, to make it part of ourselves. The Greatest News of All, the News of Christmas Day, is very difficult indeed to take in, unless we make a slow, conscious, deliberate effort to make it part of ourselves. The God of the Galaxies is also the God of the Manger. The Maker of the Universe is also the Maker of contented little baby noises as He lies in Mary's arms in Bethlehem. And He did all this for us: not for humanity in general; not for emperors, kings and presidents; not for the noble, the good, the rich and the brilliant ... but for you and for me. Christmas Day means that God cares for every individual sinner who needs His love and His forgiveness.

On Christmas Day God is telling you and me: "You may not think much of yourselves, but this is how much I think of You. I would go anywhere to be with you, and to bring You back to Myself, because I love you so much. I have come to this stable to find you; I shall go on looking for you at Calvary. Through the agony of the Cross, and triumph of the Resurrection, incarnate or glorious, I shall love you and search for you forever — *and My search shall not fail.*"

The Angel came to Mary; Mary came to Bethlehem; God came into His world; and as a result new life came within reach of all who will accept it.

It is part of the nature of God to move irresistibly closer to those who need Him. Sin is an evil and destructive force — the worst kind of disease and decay — its nature is to drive things away from God and from one another. God is the Infinitely Greater Force, the Ultimate Force, which brings people and things back together and holds them secure in Eternal and Infinite Love.

Christmas is Reconciliation Day: Armistice Day for sinful rebels. "Come home, my lost sheep," cries God. "Come home for Christmas, my prodigal sons. Gomer and Rahab, come home, my daughters. Your Father is waiting here in this stable with a Gift that brings love, welcome and restoration."

Christmas is Restoration Day, when God makes all things new — as new and as perfect as the Child in the Manger. Let us all come home rejoicing in our Father's Love.

Prayer

Lord of All, and Child in the Manger, help us to understand the true message of Christmas. Show us, most loving Lord, the Holy Mysteries of Your Incarnation at Bethlehem, that understanding their message of forgiveness and reconciliation, we may return to You in true penitence, and receive the Christmas Blessing of Everlasting Life. We ask it for the sake of Him who was born to Mary, Jesus Christ our Lord. Amen.

Easter

Some of my most senior readers may still just remember the celebrations at the end of the First World War, and I myself can recall the rejoicings in the street at the end of World War II. There is striving, strain and struggle throughout the universe: no baby is brought into the world without a woman's labour; no child learns to read, write and count without effort — its own and its teacher's! No examinations are passed without some toil; no job interview is undertaken without a certain amount of stress; no illness is defeated without struggle; no battle of any kind — moral or military — is won without effort, cost and sacrifice.

When I first began teaching in the 'fifties our school motto was *nil sine labore* — nothing without work — and it's true. The greater the achievement, the more important the victory, the greater its cost.

It is inevitable, therefore, that the Greatest of All Victories should demand the Highest of All Costs.

When the deepest mystic, the most learned theologian, the wisest philosopher and the simplest saint have all told us everything they know about the Meaning of the Cross, still we shall not understand a tiny fraction of all that Christ did for us there.

I know only this: it was the Greatest of All Victories. Life conquered death; Good defeated evil; Holiness threw down sin; Yes overcame no; Order destroyed chaos; and Love vanquished hatred. Easter Day is Victory Day — the Celebration of Christ's Supremacy: and we're all invited to His Feast.

Poem

There is nothing without struggle;
No achievement without pain;
And the fiercest rage of battle
Brings the warrior greatest gain.

From the gallant mother's labour
Comes the babe she holds so dear;
From the swimmer's aching muscles
Comes the coastline ever near.

From the smoke and blood of battle
Comes the tyrant's overthrow;
From the scholar's midnight labour
Comes new truth for all to know.

From the cross upon the hillside
Comes the resurrection morn;
Where the Greatest of All Fighters
Shows His children their New Dawn.

God of Battles, God of Victory,
God of Glory, God of Power —
Here we kneel in breathless wonder
At Your Easter Triumph Hour.

Prayer

Wonderful Resurrected Lord of Life, Conqueror of All,
grant us the grace to give our lives and hearts to You
on this Easter Victory Day. Amen.

Ascension Day

A tale is told of a simple, rural Priest who was perplexed and disturbed by the confusing and controversial theories concerning life after death which are currently fashionable in some theological colleges. The Priest was walking pensively through his Churchyard, meditating on the mysteries of Heaven, when he came across his old sexton digging a grave. "What are your views on life after death, Sam?" asked the Priest. Without a second's hesitation the old man replied with the words of the Creed: "I believe in the resurrection of the body." The Priest brightened visibly: "And so do I," he said happily, as his perplexity left him. That sound old doctrine by no means precludes the survival of our immortal souls, but it does remind us that we are not to survive as vague, feeble, disembodied, sub-personal, psychic entities. Heaven always offers much, much *more* — never less. We shall have resurrection bodies, right enough, but they will be unimaginably wonderful — and powerful beyond our wildest dreams.

Sadly, it is fashionable in some scholarly Church circles to be less than enthusiastic about the historical reality of our Lord's Ascension, but I fail to see any difficulties. For a number of days after His resurrection, Jesus appeared to the overjoyed disciples. He could come and go at will, but His resurrection body was nevertheless solid and substantial: Thomas could feel the nail prints in the Lord's hands; He ate fish and honeycomb; His strong fingers broke bread at

Emmaus in the characteristic way that Cleopas and his friend recognized. A baby can do a thousand things that an embryo cannot. An adult human being can do a thousand things which a baby cannot. A divinely resurrected body can do a thousand things which a mortal body cannot. There is nothing odd or unnatural about that kind of progression.

Jesus, our resurrected Lord, is the Pioneer, the First Commando to storm the citadel of death, and in His track we shall look with wonder at its irreparably shattered gates. Let us rejoice on this special occasion as we recall how He Who rose from the grave also ascended to His Heavenly Home.

Prayer

Truly ascended, yet ever-present Lord, grant us the grace to accept every part of Your Divine Truth, and grant us the faith which knows for certain that one day You will return in glory and in judgement with all Your holy Angels, just as You ascended to glory long ago to be our Advocate with the Father.

May the Holy Spirit guard us, guide us and protect us from every temptation and sin, so that at Your return, Lord Jesus, we shall be able to welcome You, not because we have any virtue or merit, but because Your Grace is sufficient for us.

We ask it in and through Your precious Name. Amen.

Whitsun

Before our Lord completed his work on earth and ascended to rejoin His Father in glory, He promised that He would not leave us comfortless. He promised that the Holy Spirit, the Paraclete, the Strengthener and Comforter would come to us.

There is no greater certainty than that Christ's promises will be fulfilled. Whatever else in the universe may appear to us to be shrouded in doubt, difficulty, mystery and uncertainty, the Word of God and the Promises of Christ are totally reliable and unshakeably steadfast. Jesus gave us the Promise, and the Holy Spirit has most assuredly come.

As we think of Whitsun, or Pentecost, as a special occasion, we need to remind ourselves of Who the Holy Spirit really is, and the miracles that He is always so willing and able to accomplish for us — if only we will invite Him into our lives.

The Holy Spirit is the Third Person of the Divine Trinity. He is God, just as the Father and the Son are God. He is another Supra-Personality, in exactly the same way that They are. He was as closely involved in our creation as the other Two Persons were. He is as concerned with loving and sustaining us today as the other Two Persons are. We are *thrice* blessed: we have a Father, a Saviour and a Comforter.

The specific work of the Holy Spirit is to inspire us, guide us, strengthen, comfort and help us, as we go about the day-to-day business of living. He is our constant Renewer, Energizer and Healer. He gives us gifts of power and gifts of character.

It is the Living Power of the Holy Spirit which enables some members of Christ's flock to prophesy, and others to teach; some to preach, and others to speak in tongues or to interpret them. Some work miracles of faith, while others heal in His Name. It is the Power of the Holy Spirit which makes cowards into heroes; drunkards and drug addicts into men and women with iron-willed self-control; the sad and the despairing into the confident and the joyful; the vicious, the spiteful and the aggressive into gentle, peaceful companions; swaggering, boastful, ambitious egotists into quiet, modest unassuming friends of the poor and the rejected; philanderers and adulterers into loving and faithful marriage partners; thieves into honest and trustworthy men and women; and misers into open-hearted, open-handed philanthropists ... *There is nothing the Holy Spirit cannot accomplish.*

We celebrate the special occasion of Whitsun, because it is the Day He came to us nearly 2000 years ago: yet His tongues of fire still ignite God's people today, and His rushing mighty wind still blows all evil to destruction before it.

Prayer

Holy Spirit, on this Whitsun Day we pray especially for Your help. Come among us with Your love, Your power and grace. Bring us Your miracles of healing and restoration. Grant us peace and joy. Inspire our thoughts, our words and our deeds so that every part of our lives acknowledges and expresses Your purity and truth.

Lift our inadequate human worship to the very gate of Heaven, and to Your Throne, that together with the Father and the Son You may be pleased with our humble prayers and simple praises. Bathe us in the purifying flames of Your Power until all that is selfish and unworthy is taken from us. Remake us as what You would have us be, because what You will for us is always what is best for us.

Fill our lives so completely with the knowledge and love of God that we shall recognize every moment, every hour and every day as a special occasion because You are with us.

We ask it in the name of Him Who promised that You would come to us, Jesus our Lord. Amen.